ATTACK ON PEARL HARBOR

THE TRUE STORY OF THE DAY AMERICA ENTERED WORLD WAR II

ISBN 0-439-33596-5

Text, Design, Illustrations, and Compilation © 2001 by The Madison Press Limited.
All rights reserved.
Published by Scholastic Inc., 555 Broadway, New York, NY 10012,
by arrangement with Madison Press Books.
SCHOLASTIC and associated logos are trademarks and/or
registered trademarks of Scholastic Inc.

13 12 11   6 7 8/0

Printed in the U.S.A.   40

First Scholastic printing, September 2002

Book Design: Jason Ulrich
Project Research/Interviews: John Treiber

ATTACK ON PEARL HARBOR

THE TRUE STORY OF THE DAY AMERICA ENTERED WORLD WAR II

Text by Shelley Tanaka • Paintings by David Craig
Maps by Jack McMaster • Historical consultation by John Lundstrom

SCHOLASTIC INC.

New York Toronto London Auckland Sydney
Mexico City New Delhi Hong Kong Buenos Aires

There Could Be War

A carefree Peter Nottage at the window of the family Buick.

Peter Nottage shoved his surfboard into the back of the family Buick. His black cocker spaniel, Baby Girl, bounced and sniffed, as she always did when she saw the car being packed.

It was December 6, 1941. Finally Saturday morning, and Peter could toss his shoes into the back of his closet for the weekend. That was the only problem with being in the seventh grade at Punahou School in Honolulu. Starting in the seventh grade, students had to wear shoes.

But shoes just got in the way of all the things you had to do when you lived in Hawaii. Like swimming in Manoa Stream and racing leaf boats in the pond below the falls. Or hiking through the woods looking for kukui nuts. All the boys liked to polish them up with breadfruit leaves to make slides for their Boy Scout neckerchiefs.

And you certainly didn't need shoes on Waikiki Beach, where there was always plenty to do. Swim, surf, canoe, race crabs, or just sit and stare at the rich tourists at the Royal Hawaiian Hotel. Most of all, Peter loved to watch the Hawaiian fishermen bring in their catch. Sometimes

SURF RIDING, HAWAII

A TROPICAL PARADISE

A gentle climate, sparkling beaches, and lush plant life made the Hawaiian Islands an exotic paradise. Sugar cane and pineapple plantations were common sights as were the tourists who came to enjoy the sand and surf. Among the famous landmarks not far from Pearl Harbor were Waikiki Beach, the Royal Hawaiian Hotel, and the peninsula called Diamond Head (above left). Servicemen stationed in Hawaii sent postcards like these home.

OAHU AND PEARL HARBOR

Oahu is one of the Hawaiian Islands, which in 1941 were a U.S. Territory. Hawaiians called Pearl Harbor "Wai Momi" or "pearl waters" because of the pearl oysters that once thrived there. The natural sheltered bay at the southern end of Oahu made an excellent naval harbor. In May 1940, President Roosevelt moved the main base of the U.S. fleet from southern California to Pearl Harbor. "Battleship Row" was the name given to the line of battleships (each named after a state) moored along the southeast shore of Ford Island in the center of Pearl Harbor (inset map).

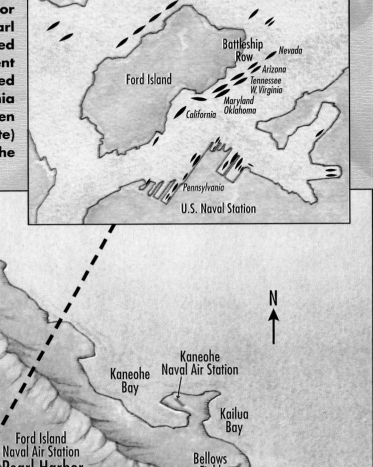

they gave him free fish if he helped pull in the nets. Ever since the fourth grade, Mrs. Pukui had been teaching the Punahou students all about Hawaiian culture. She had told them how her ancestors had first come to the islands from the south, crossing thousands of miles of open sea in swift sail-rigged canoes. The Hawaiians came from a long line of expert fishermen and boatsmen.

Mrs. Nottage came out of the house with the family's Japanese maid, Fumie, who was carrying a pile of beach towels. Peter's mother frowned when she saw the surfboard leaning against the backseat, but Peter was too excited to notice. The Nottages were going to spend the weekend with friends. Mr. and Mrs. Mitchell had an elegant old home on Kaneohe Bay, just a forty-five-minute drive from Honolulu.

Peter loved visiting the Mitchells. Not only was there first-rate surfing at nearby Kailua Bay, but there was also a big naval air station right across the bay from the Mitchell house. He had heard that the Navy had a whole new fleet of seaplanes stationed there, and he couldn't wait to see them. These days you could often watch planes practicing their maneuvers and drills all over the island. Sometimes the fliers even shot at one another with fake smoke.

Peter in his aloha shirt, the favorite garb of islanders.

Peter knew why there was so much activity on the local bases. He had heard the grown-ups talking about a possible war with Japan. Even now, the Japanese ambassadors were in Washington, trying to come to an agreement that would keep both countries out of the war.

It was true that many of Peter's friends were Japanese Americans whose parents had come to Hawaii many years before to work on the sugar cane and pineapple plantations. But they were just the buddies he swapped homework with or played baseball with.

They were hardly the enemy.

Commander Mitsuo Fuchida was worried. He stood on the bridge of the aircraft carrier *Akagi* and carefully scanned the gray Pacific Ocean. The six carriers of the Japanese fleet had reduced speed so they could take on fuel one last time. If the refueling was successful, the fleet would push south to Hawaii, where Fuchida and his pilots were planning to change the course of history. In twenty-four hours, they would launch a surprise air attack on Pearl Harbor, dropping bombs and torpedoes on the Pacific base of the U.S. Navy.

The daring of it still took his breath away.

He knew it was an extremely dangerous mission. In order to cross the ocean to Hawaii, the fleet had to refuel twice on the high seas — a risky operation unless the water was calm. And penetrating Pearl Harbor itself would be no easy task. The entrance was narrow and well patrolled, and the harbor was extremely shallow. Normal torpedoes dropped from the air

Commander Mitsuo Fuchida, leader of the air attack on Pearl Harbor.

would get stuck in the muddy bottom before they had a chance to move forward.

The Japanese hoped they had solved this problem. They had invented a torpedo with special wooden fins that allowed it to be launched in shallow water. But the torpedoes only worked if the planes came in very low and at a very slow speed, making them an easy target for antiaircraft guns.

Fuchida scanned the skies, looking for signs of American planes while the refueling operation took place. The Japanese were well within the area patrolled by the United States each day. If the fleet were sighted, it would head straight back to Japan. The mission would be canceled, and all those months of training and preparation would be for nothing.

Route of the Japanese attack

THE RISING SUN

In 1941, far away from the Hawaiian Islands, the world was already at war. By the summer of 1940, Germany, under the leadership of Adolf Hitler, had overrun Poland, Norway, Denmark, France, Belgium, Holland, and Luxembourg. Britain stood alone. Japan had a pact called the Tripartite Agreement with Germany and Italy, making the three countries allies. Japan had invaded China. Britain and European countries had colonies in the Pacific that were in danger of takeover by Japan because they had the oil and other natural resources needed by Japan for its continued expansion. The United States controlled the Philippines, and these islands lay across the route to the Dutch, British, and French colonies.

The United States was against Japan's expansion into this part of the world. When President Roosevelt imposed bans on the export of fuels, steel, and scrap metal to Japan, a confrontation between America and Japan seemed sure to happen.

The refueling was finally finished. The oil tankers turned around and headed for safer waters. Then the fleet picked up speed and raced toward Pearl Harbor.

Fuchida knew his airmen were ready. He just hoped the submarine force could also do its job. The naval high command had given the air attack only a fifty percent chance of success. To provide additional firepower, submarines were approaching Hawaii from the south at this very moment.

Fuchida thought the submarine plan was too risky. It would only take one glimpse of a Japanese sub near the harbor to put the Americans on full alert. And if that happened, his planes would be shot out of the sky like passing ducks.

Ensign Kazuo Sakamaki lay in his narrow bunk on the large submarine *I-24*, off the south coast of Oahu. In a few hours he would embark on the mission of his life. This is what he had been waiting for ever since the day he had entered the Japanese Naval Academy at the age of nineteen. For four years he had gone through brutal physical training. He had rowed a cutter until his hands bled; charged a boat into the fiercest storm, even when he was sick and vomiting. He had learned how to pull himself off the floor for another wrestling bout when he could scarcely breathe through his exhaustion.

He had studied hard in the classroom as well, learning everything about military life. Most of all, he had learned that nothing could be more honorable than dying gloriously in

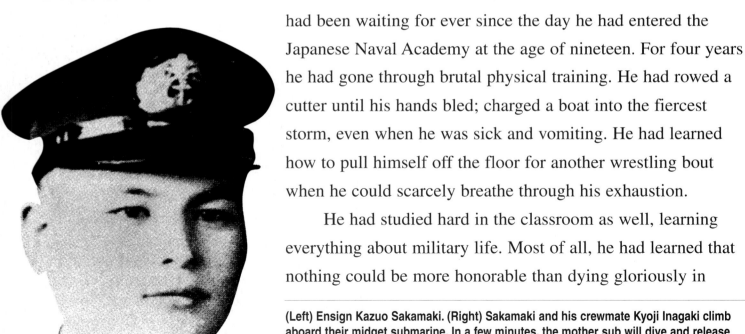

(Left) Ensign Kazuo Sakamaki. (Right) Sakamaki and his crewmate Kyoji Inagaki climb aboard their midget submarine. In a few minutes, the mother sub will dive and release their sub underwater.

battle, like the samurai warriors of old.

Within one year of graduating, Sakamaki had quickly risen to become a midget-submarine captain in the Special Attack Forces. His assignments became more purposeful, more specific. He spent hours memorizing the layout of every major harbor on the Pacific. He practiced steering a midget submarine through a narrow, shallow inlet in the dead of night.

Then, only three weeks ago, he had finally found out what he had been training for. Japan was going to war with the United States, and the Special Forces would be part of the first attack.

Sakamaki's squadron was made up of five midget submarines. Each one was carried piggyback on the afterdeck of a mother sub. The mini subs and their two-man crews would be released just outside Pearl Harbor. They would sneak through the channel at night and lie in wait until dawn. Then they would aim their torpedoes at the biggest prizes in the harbor — the eight U.S. battleships that were moored there.

Sakamaki knew that once the midgets were inside the harbor, they would be trapped like fish in a bucket. He would not likely come back from his mission alive. His father had named him Kazuo, peace boy. Now he would give his life for his country and for peace.

He got up from his bunk. He wrote a last letter to his father, saying good-bye. He carefully packed up his belongings so they could be returned to his parents after his death. He included a lock of his hair and a clipping from one of his fingernails. He washed, dressed, and tied on his

The ship's wheel (1) and gyrocompass (2), located in the control room of the midget sub.

white *hachimaki*, the samurai's headband. Then he opened the small bottle of perfume he had bought on his last night in Japan. He sprayed the perfume on his body, just as Japanese warriors had always done.

Sakamaki reported for final instructions. The captain looked at him with concern. They both knew Sakamaki had been having trouble with his gyrocompass, which would make it difficult to direct the sub when it was underwater.

"Ensign Sakamaki, we have arrived at our destination, but your gyrocompass is not working. What are you going to do?"

Sakamaki did not hesitate. He could not quit now when he was so close to his goal. He could see the red and green lights of Honolulu in the distance. The target was right in front of him, only ten miles away. How could he miss?

"Captain, I am going ahead."

"On to Pearl Harbor!" the captain shouted.

"On to Pearl Harbor!"

George DeLong glanced at his watch as the bus made its way from Honolulu to Pearl Harbor. It was only 11:00 p.m. Saturday night. He'd be back on his ship well before the midnight curfew.

He had just been to a movie in town. It was a Chinese or Japanese film, he wasn't even sure which, and he had been the only sailor in the

Nineteen-year-old George DeLong, a seaman aboard the USS *Oklahoma*.

13

place, but he didn't care. It was his night off, and he just enjoyed being on his own. He liked wandering through downtown Honolulu, hearing the shreds of different languages, breathing in the smells of exotic spices and foods drifting from the shops and alleys. It was a far cry from Annville, Pennsylvania, the small town where he had grown up.

George took a deep breath of balmy sea air. Life was good. He was nineteen years old, a quartermaster striker on the USS *Oklahoma*, one of the great old battleships of the Pacific Fleet. He had only been in the Navy for a year, but so far he loved everything about it. He didn't even mind boot training — the drills, sleeping in ice-cold barracks to get used to conditions at sea. It had all been new and exciting.

Now his home was a cramped bunk in the bottom of a giant warship. His new family were the shipmates that he lived and worked with.

The routine wasn't tough. The ship spent one week at sea doing maneuvers, then came home to Pearl for a week. The time in port was pretty relaxed, with half the crew on shore at any given time. Hawaii was a great place to be stationed, and Honolulu was one big party.

At the harbor, George stepped aboard the motor launch that would take the sailors back to their ships.

A few of the guys were a little the worse for wear after an evening of barhopping. Yet somehow they managed to climb the ladders onto their ships without falling into the water.

George reached the main deck of the *Okie* and looked out over the harbor. The big ships of the U.S. fleet were lined up in pairs. It was rare to see so many on Battleship Row. Usually some were kept out at sea for training. The ships looked like floating gray fortresses with their thick towering masts and their battle guns poised.

If war came, and there were rumors this might be soon, the mighty American fleet would be ready.

George made his way down to his sleeping quarters in the emergency steering room. It was a small compartment filled with four huge steering wheels that could be used to turn the ship if the bridge were destroyed in battle. Eight bunks had been built above the wheels. George's was at the top. He undressed, said good-night to his roommates, and climbed up into bed. He was planning to sleep in the next morning. After all, it was Sunday — the slackest day of the whole week.

Crewmen looked forward to going ashore on leave (opposite) and enjoying the scenic wonders of the Hawaiian Islands (above).

PART TWO
The Attack

Commander Mitsuo Fuchida woke up before dawn. It was Sunday morning, December 7, 1941. He put on his flying uniform. The hem crinkled where his wife had sewn prayers into the seam. Beneath his jacket he wore a red shirt. If he were hit, the other pilots would not be able to see the blood and become discouraged at the sight of their wounded leader. He thought about his eight-year-old son and four-year-old daughter at home in Japan. He knew he might never see them again.

The planes had been checked and rechecked. They were ready to go. The scouts had reported that a large part of the U.S. fleet was in Pearl Harbor for the weekend. The aircraft carriers, the most valuable targets, were out at sea, but there were still ninety-four vessels in port, including eight battleships.

On the *Akagi*'s flight deck, dozens of planes were lined up wingtip to wingtip and nose to tail. The ship rolled and

A Japanese dive bomber makes the dangerous takeoff from the carrier.

Fuchida salutes as his level bomber prepares to take off.

heaved, and Fuchida could see whitecapped waves licking up from the black water. The crews were already drenched with sea spray as they held on to their planes in the strong wind.

If these were practice maneuvers, they would never attempt to launch aircraft in such rough seas. But these were not maneuvers. Even if they lost several planes during takeoff, the operation would still go ahead.

One by one the pilots climbed into the cockpits and waved good-bye. Fuchida saluted his officers and walked to the plane that he shared with his pilot and radioman. As he was about to climb up, a crew chief handed him a *hachimaki*, a special gift from the maintenance teams.

Fuchida tied the white headband around his flying cap. He checked his equipment. The Japanese pilots did not wear parachutes. If they were hit in battle, they would release their bombs and go down with their planes.

The six carriers turned into the wind. The battle flag was hoisted, and the planes shook as their engines warmed up. The men on the decks waved their caps.

(Top) The carrier *Akagi*. (Middle) Japanese crewmen make final preparations for takeoff. (Bottom) A Japanese painting shows how the planes were stored on the carriers with their wings folded.

The engine of the first plane roared as it started its run down the length of the carrier, slowly gaining speed. Fuchida held his breath as the carrier heaved up dangerously on the waves, then watched in relief as the plane left the deck just as the ship pitched down.

The next plane was already moving forward. The crews on the six carriers cheered loudly as each of the 183 planes took off. They circled once over the fleet and then headed south toward Pearl Harbor, only the signal lights of the lead planes piercing the black sky.

Kazuo Sakamaki didn't know what to do. He was in his midget submarine just outside Pearl Harbor. It was still dark, but something was wrong. Not only was his gyrocompass not working, but now the sub kept bobbing up and down, trying to rise to the surface.

THE MIDGET SUBMARINE

Sakamaki and Inagaki piloted a two-man "Type A" midget submarine that was seventy-eight feet long, weighed forty-six tons, and was propelled by battery-powered motors. But the gyrocompass was not working properly, making it difficult to direct the sub. Sakamaki also had problems keeping the sub on an even keel.

A submarine's depth in the water is controlled by tanks inside the sub that are filled with either air or water. When the tanks are filled with air, the ship is lighter and will rise to the surface. When the tanks are filled with water, the ship is heavier and able to stay underwater.

To keep the sub at the right depth and on an even keel, the two men took turns crawling on their stomachs along the cramped tunnel that led forward and aft of the control room, shifting ballast or weight, and turning the dials that filled the tanks with the right amount of air or water. Sakamaki and Inagaki could not complete their mission with a crippled submarine.

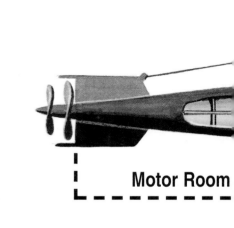

Motor Room

If the submarine broke through the water, it might be spotted by the enemy, and the entire mission would be a failure.

For hours now, Sakamaki and his crewman, Kyoji Inagaki, had been taking turns wriggling from one end of the sub to the other, moving ballast to correct the trim. The inside tunnel was very narrow, and it took a long time.

Again Sakamaki started to move the sub forward. Then he brought it up slightly and looked through the periscope.

They were going in the wrong direction!

His hands slippery with sweat, he changed direction again and again, trying to aim the sub toward the mouth of the harbor. But nothing seemed to work.

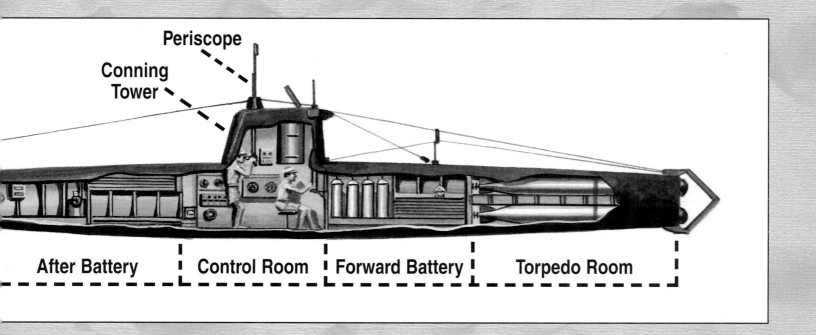

Periscope

Conning Tower

After Battery | Control Room | Forward Battery | Torpedo Room

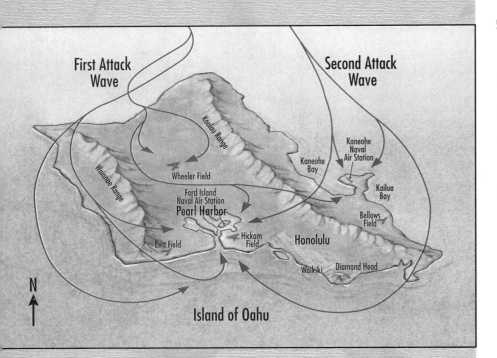

First Attack Wave

Second Attack Wave

Koolau Range

Waianae Range

Wheeler Field

Kaneohe Naval Air Station

Kaneohe Bay

Ford Island Naval Air Station

Pearl Harbor

Kailua Bay

Bellows Field

Ewa Field

Hickam Field

Honolulu

Waikiki

Diamond Head

N

Island of Oahu

THE AIR ATTACK

The Japanese air attack came in two waves. The first wave of 183 planes began its attack at 7:55 a.m. It was a complete surprise. The attacking force of torpedo bombers, dive bombers, level bombers, and fighters split up to hit the U.S. fleet and the airfields at the same time. The Navy air bases at Ford Island and Kaneohe Bay, the Marine airfield at Ewa, and the Army Air Corps fields at Bellows, Wheeler, and Hickam were all hit, along with the ships moored at Pearl Harbor. With its planes destroyed, the United States could not intercept the Japanese planes. The second attack wave came at 8:50 a.m. These 170 planes concentrated on Pearl Harbor and Kaneohe Naval Air Station. The entire attack ended shortly before 10:00 a.m., less than two hours after it had begun.

Sakamaki again peeked through the periscope. Ahead of him lay the entrance to Pearl Harbor, guarded by two U.S. destroyers. The ships were so close, he could see the white uniforms of the sailors on board.

It was now or never.

Sakamaki took a deep breath and pointed his sub toward the U.S. ships.

Commander Fuchida was flying over thick clouds, leading a group of forty-nine level bombers. On either side were the other groups of attackers — forty torpedo planes, fifty-one dive bombers, and forty-three fighter planes.

Dawn began to break, and a brilliant red sun filled the eastern sky, lighting up the clouds below. He opened the cockpit and saw the formation of planes all around him, their wings sparkling. It was a glorious sight. He raised his arms and waved at his fellow pilots, and they waved back.

Fuchida switched on the radio and tuned in to an early-morning Honolulu station. He adjusted his course slightly and headed toward the broadcast.

They were getting close.

Suddenly, the clouds parted like a curtain. The northern tip of the island lay straight ahead. Directly south was Pearl Harbor and the air and marine bases that surrounded it. To the east was the Kaneohe Naval Air Station, another target.

"*Tenkai!*" he ordered. "Take attack positions!" Pearl Harbor was clearly visible, glistening in the sun.

The four groups split apart to make their final approaches. Dive bombers cut across the island and

This photo taken from a Japanese plane shows the first moments of the attack over Pearl Harbor.

headed for Kaneohe. Fighter planes snaked a zigzag path toward Wheeler Field. Others circled to come over Hickam Air Force Base. But Fuchida and his level bombers curled around the southwest tip of the island and headed right for Pearl Harbor.

Fuchida scanned the sky for American planes. He could see none. There was no sign of antiaircraft activity from the ground. The radio station continued to play music. The ships in the harbor were gray and still.

He knew the mission would be a success. The Japanese had caught Pearl Harbor sleeping.

He ordered the radio man to send out the code message to say that the attack was a surprise: *Tora, tora, tora.*

"Notify all planes to launch attacks," he added.

The group of dive bombers swooped down over the air bases, where U.S. planes were lined up in tidy rows. They released their bombs, and huge billows of black smoke rose from the ground. Within minutes the torpedo planes and level bombers began their run at the battleships. They came straight in, nice and low, just as they had practiced.

(Opposite) Fires rage as Battleship Row comes under heavy attack. (Above) Torpedo tracks lead to USS *West Virginia* and *Oklahoma*. The concentric rings in the water show a near miss. The smoke in the background is from bombing at Hickam Field.

On the USS *Oklahoma*, George DeLong opened his eyes and swung his legs over the side of his bunk. It was 7:50 a.m. He was glad he had decided to skip breakfast. He would get up, have a shower. He had the day off, but the crew was getting ready for a big inspection. He would help the guys with the final cleaning. Then the rest of the day would be free. Maybe he would go down to Waikiki Beach and rent a horse. He loved to ride along the edge of the sand, the palm trees overhead, the trade winds bathing his face.

Below the bunks, some of the men were already at work. One sailor was swabbing the red linoleum with a mop and a bucket of soapy water.

George started to climb down from his bunk.

All of a sudden, he heard the crackle of the loudspeaker: "All hands, man your battle stations and set watertight conditions!"

George yawned. Why were they having a drill on a Sunday morning? He and the other men in the compartment shrugged and continued with what they were doing.

The loudspeaker came on again almost immediately. This time the voice swore, something George had never heard before.

"Hey! Real planes, real bombs! Man your battle stations! This is no —"

The voice was interrupted by an explosion, and then another one.

They were under attack!

A bove the *Oklahoma,* the sky was filled with planes dropping torpedoes and bombs. Billows of smoke and flying debris exploded from the ground and the spit of gunfire filled the air. Fuchida's plane banked sharply, and his level bombers followed him in precise single-file formation right over Battleship Row.

All at once the American forces came to life as the shipboard guns below let loose. The sky was filled with antiaircraft fire. Fuchida's plane jerked, as if it had been struck by a huge club. The fuselage had been hit, but the plane was still under control.

Ignoring the shells bursting all around them, Fuchida's planes circled and came in again.

There was a huge explosion below. A giant column of dark-red fire and smoke rose high into the sky, making his plane shudder from the afterblast. It was the *Arizona.* A bomb had hit her powder magazine, and the battleship had exploded in flames.

Fuchida's planes circled and headed into the antiaircraft fire once more. He

THE *ARIZONA'S* DESTRUCTION

At 8:10 a.m., a bomb hit the *Arizona*'s forward ammunition magazine or storage area and then exploded (1), setting off more than a million pounds of gunpowder (2). The explosion and fire killed 1,177 crewmen. Broken in two, and with its bridge and foremast toppled (3), the battleship sank in less than nine minutes (4).

grasped the bomb release handle, held his breath, and let go.

He lay on his stomach and peered through the slot in the floor of the plane. It was like looking down a long tunnel. The bombs grew smaller and smaller as they fell. Finally they looked as small as poppy seeds.

If the bombs missed the ship, waterspouts would create huge rings in the water. But if they hit the target, there would be only tiny flashes of smoke.

Fuchida counted two rings — and two flashes.

"Two hits!" he shouted triumphantly. He ordered the rest of his bombers to return to the carriers. He would stay behind to survey the damage. Then he would take the good news back to his superiors.

On the *Oklahoma*, George DeLong heard a deafening clang as the watertight door above them slammed shut. The crew was just following orders by closing all the openings in the ship, but now the sailors in the steering room were trapped.

The ship jerked up and rocked from side to side. George grabbed onto the nearest bunk. Then the whole ship seemed to groan and started to turn over. The bucket of soapy water spilled, and one sailor lost his footing and slid up against the bulkhead. Loose machinery, lockers, and engine parts began to shift and roll with a tremendous rattle and crash.

George scrambled back up into his bunk to avoid being crushed. But the ship kept rolling until he was clinging to his bunk, almost upside down. He wondered whether he was about to die.

The ship rolled almost completely over and stopped. Then all the lights went out, and the room was pitch black.

The Mitchell household was still asleep when Peter Nottage woke up. He slipped on a pair of shorts and an aloha shirt and went outside. Baby Girl shook herself awake and padded over to join him.

The house was built on a high bluff that overlooked Kaneohe Bay. Across the water, the air station looked pretty quiet. Peter could see the two new hangars that housed the Navy's seaplanes. Most of the planes were neatly lined up on the ramp outside. Four planes were floating at anchor in the bay.

Peter heard a drone behind him. He looked up, and three silvery planes appeared above his head, coming in right over the house from the west. They were flying very close together and very low. He could see the goggled faces of the pilots.

Peter had never seen planes like these before. They weren't the usual P-26 fighters with the open cockpits, or even the sharp-nosed P-40s. Each plane had a big red circle painted on the underside of each wing. As he watched, the planes swerved over the bay and disappeared to the north.

Within minutes they swooped in again. This time they sprayed machine-gun fire. Peter

(Left) Peter on the Mitchell dock earlier in 1941.
(Opposite) Peter and Mr. Mitchell witness the attack on Kaneohe Naval Air Station.

could see the water jump as the bullets splashed into the bay.

Wow, he thought. This was great. The Navy was holding maneuvers right before his eyes. Must be the red team's planes against the blue team.

The door opened behind him and Mr. Mitchell came out, still wearing his pajamas. He squinted as a group of nine planes came in over the air station.

"Never seen one of those," he said. "What kind of plane do you suppose that is, Peter?"

"I don't know. I guess — "

One of the planes dropped a bomb right on the ramp of the seaplane hangar, setting it on fire. Metal, concrete, and glass exploded from the ground.

Peter started. Had one of the Navy pilots gone crazy? Somebody was really going to get it for that.

And then one of the seaplanes anchored in the bay was hit, and it blew up in a burst of fire.

Kaneohe was suddenly a sea of smoke and flames. All the seaplanes seemed to be burning. Thick black smoke began to pour from one of the buildings. Alarms brayed.

A group of fighter planes swooped in again, but this time they faced fire from below. One of the attacking planes seemed to be hit. The pilot turned and waggled his wings at the rest of his squadron, which broke formation and peeled off. He came in alone, heading right for the station armory, as straight and deliberate as an arrow. Then, as Peter watched, the plane slammed into the ground and burst into flames.

Peter's mother flung open the door behind them. "It's on the radio. It's war!" she shouted. "Those are the Japanese! We're under attack!" And she grabbed Peter's arm and yanked him into the house.

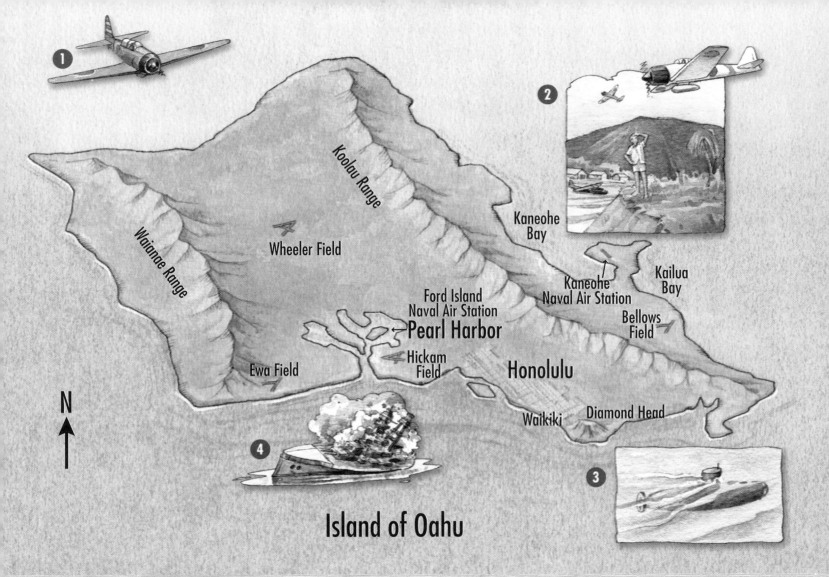

Island of Oahu

THAT SUNDAY MORNING

(Clockwise from top): Commander Fuchida (1) flies over Oahu in a three-man level bomber to attack Pearl Harbor. Peter Nottage witnesses the first wave of the attack as it hits Kaneohe Naval Air Station (2). Ensign Sakamaki tries to correct his sub's course but ends up heading away from the harbor (3). George DeLong is trapped inside as the listing USS *Oklahoma* (4) begins to capsize.

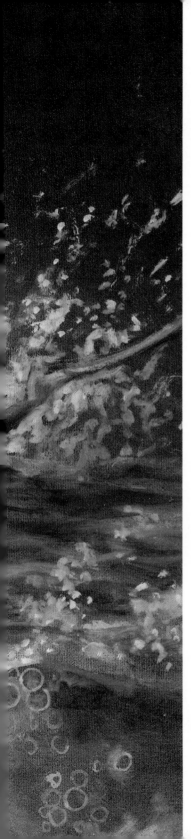

In the emergency steering room of the *Oklahoma*, someone turned on a flashlight and shone it around the compartment. George DeLong's heart sank. Sea water was pouring in through the air vent, filling the room. The water was lapping at his ankles, then his knees. The compartment would be completely flooded in minutes if they didn't do something quickly.

"Get the clothes out of the lockers!" someone shouted. Everyone grabbed whatever clothing they could — some even peeling off their pants and shirts — and tried to stuff it into the vent hole.

But it was no use. The hole was big, and the clothes just blew out again.

"Get one of the bunk mattresses!"

It was a brilliant idea. They rolled up a mattress and stuffed it into the vent like a cork. The mattress was just the right size, and though water was still seeping out of the corners, it was no longer gushing into the compartment.

The problem was that it took four of them to hold the mattress in place. They looked around. Willard Beal was only seventeen, but he was the biggest, heaviest guy in the room.

"Beal, sit on top of the mattress," someone ordered, and he did.

Still the water kept rising. It was soon up to Beal's waist. And it was getting higher.

"You guys better get something else," he hollered, "because the water

George DeLong uses a wrench to bang out SOS as the water continues to rise.

is up to my chest!"

Just then, like a miniature life raft, a game board floated on the water toward them. Someone snatched it up and placed it on top of the mattress. Then a length of rope floated by, just long enough to lash the board down by securing it to the pipes around the air duct.

Now the water was still trickling in, but they had stopped the immediate danger.

George and the others climbed up to the highest point they could reach and sat down. They turned off the flashlight to conserve the battery. Then they all tried to think of what to do next. How could they get out of the compartment?

They couldn't. They were trapped in a black, airtight room, the rising water licking at their knees. It was like being in a coffin, buried under the sea. If the water rose much farther,

(Above) The crew of the *California* abandons ship as burning oil surrounds it. (Below) The destroyer *Shaw*, in floating dry dock south of Battleship Row, is hit and explodes toward the end of the attack.

THE DESTRUCTION: BATTLESHIP ROW

Within the first minutes of the attack, all of the battleships lying along Ford Island were hit by bombs or torpedoes. The *West Virginia* (right and below) sank quickly. The *Oklahoma* capsized and sank. The *Arizona* exploded and sank in less than nine minutes. The *California* (opposite top), *Maryland*, *Tennessee*, and *Nevada* all suffered damage.

THE DESTRUCTION: THE BASES

Wheeler Field (below), in the center of Oahu, was an important air base and a critical target for the Japanese. The Naval Air Station on Ford Island (above, left and right) suffered heavy damage, as did the base at Kaneohe Bay. While barracks and planes burned at Hickam Field (right), the American flag — shredded by machine-gun fire — still flew (inset).

they would drown. If they ran out of air, they would suffocate.

Time passed. Sounds reached them through the walls of the ship. George heard thuds and shooting. At one point he heard vibrations, like propellers in the water.

Someone found a huge wrench. George had learned Morse code at quartermaster school, and he began to bang out SOS on the side of the ship. No one knew whether anyone could hear him, but it seemed like their only chance.

S . . . O . . . S.

Someone was tapping back. Was someone coming to the rescue?

S . . . O . . . S.

Their hearts sank. The sound was coming from the next compartment. Soon SOS taps were echoing throughout the ship, bouncing off the metal walls.

Others were trapped, too, and everyone was frantically calling for help.

Kazuo Sakamaki looked through the periscope of the midget submarine. He could see great columns of black smoke rising into the sky above Pearl Harbor. The enemy ships were burning.

"They've done it!" he shouted to Inagaki. "Look at that!"

The air attack was a success. It gave them both hope. Sakamaki steered straight for the harbor. No

39

matter what the cost, he would complete his mission. He would fire his torpedoes into an enemy ship.

Suddenly there was a huge bang, and the sub stopped moving. He had run onto a coral reef. By the time he had jostled the sub off the reef, the steering mechanism was damaged, and one of their two precious torpedoes was smashed.

Now the battery was leaking. Gas and smoke were filling the sub with a bitter smell that made his throat close up and his eyes sting. He felt sick, and he was very tired. He tried again to steer the sub toward the harbor entrance. Then the ship hit a reef for the second time.

Once again he and Inagaki began slowly moving ballast from the front to the rear to raise the nose of the sub.

The overflowing batteries gave Sakamaki electric shocks as he pulled himself along with his elbows through the narrow tunnel. He got the ship afloat again, but now the second torpedo was damaged beyond repair.

There was only one thing to do. He would forge ahead and ram his sub right into an American battleship. It would mean the end for him and Inagaki, but it was the only way to salvage something out of their failed mission.

"If we can't blast the enemy battleship, we will climb onto it and kill as many men as we can," Sakamaki said. But as he headed toward the harbor for the last time, fatigue and the foul air in the sub overtook him, and he lost consciousness.

When he woke up, it was dark. Inagaki was weeping. Sakamaki began

Sakamaki and Inagaki are forced to abandon their mini sub.

Two views of the captured mini sub near Bellows Field.

to cry, too. His sub had not even made it into the harbor.

It was over. Exhausted, he steered the ship southeast toward the rendezvous point with the mother sub. Then he surfaced, opened the hatch, and collapsed into sleep as his ship bobbed along the moonlit sea.

When dawn broke, he saw land on the horizon. As he tried to run the ship toward shore, the sub suddenly trembled and went silent. White smoke and sparks spewed from the batteries, and the submarine came to a stop. It had hit another reef.

Sakamaki knew that no matter what happened, the submarine must not fall into enemy hands. It was time to destroy his own ship with the explosives they carried just for that purpose.

He lit the fuse and climbed up onto the deck. The dark waves were rising high. The shore lay about seven hundred feet away.

Sakamaki looked at his crewmate.

"I'm going now," he said, and he jumped into the water.

Inagaki jumped in right behind him.

The water was shockingly cold, and salt water filled his throat. He swam away from the sub and waited for the explosion.

There was none. He had not even been able to blow up his own ship.

In despair he tried to turn back, but he had no strength to fight the huge breakers that were pushing him toward shore. In the distance, he saw Inagaki disappear beneath the water. Then the giant waves swallowed him up.

When Sakamaki opened his eyes, he was lying on a beach staring up at a man holding a gun. The man had a Japanese face, but he was an American soldier.

Kazuo Sakamaki was now a prisoner of war.

With many homes damaged and fears of another attack, families and friends bunked together.

By 10:00 a.m., the attack was over. When the smoke had cleared at Kaneohe, the Nottages hurried to their car. Peter found a bullet on the floor — a .30 caliber from an American machine gun had gone right through the car roof.

The road to Honolulu was plugged with cars, military Jeeps, and fire trucks. It took ages to get home. Pearl Harbor had been badly bombed, and friends who lived closer to the base came to stay with the Nottages.

At 3:30 p.m., the radio announced that Hawaii was now under martial law. All lights were to be turned off at night. Residents were not to use their phones, and everyone was ordered to stay off the streets. Peter's mother filled the bathtub and sinks with water. Outside, shots rang out from time to time.

Everybody bunked together on the living-room floor that night. All the windows were covered with blankets. Peter didn't sleep much. Planes flew over the house, and the night was peppered with the sounds of gunfire and shells exploding.

There was only one thought on everyone's mind. Would the Japanese come back? Would the whole island be invaded?

PART THREE

Just the Beginning

Commander Fuchida's plane was the last one to touch down on the *Akagi*. He counted twenty-one large holes in the port side of his plane. Many of the fliers were so low on gas that they barely made it back. One plane skidded into the water before it reached the carrier, and the crew had to be pulled out of the icy ocean.

The carrier crews were already busy refueling and rearming the planes to prepare to return to Hawaii for another attack. Fuchida went to the bridge and proudly reported to his superiors. At least seven battleships had been damaged or sunk, and more than one hundred American planes had been destroyed. The Japanese had lost only twenty-nine aircraft in combat, though all five midget submarines had failed to return.

"There are still many targets that should be hit," Fuchida said. "I recommend that we launch another attack." They could take out more ships, dockyards, fuel tanks, maybe even find the U.S. carriers. Another assault, perhaps followed by an invasion of the islands, would push America completely out of the central Pacific.

To Fuchida's huge disappointment, the admiral did not agree. The mission had achieved better results than anyone had expected. But the Americans had been surprisingly quick to launch a counterattack, and they would be waiting for the Japanese to return.

No, they would stick to their original plan and not press their luck.

Fuchida and his squadron leave Pearl Harbor.

Deep within the *Oklahoma*, George DeLong had lost track of time. How long had he and the seven other sailors been down here, crammed together in the utter blackness? He no longer felt thirsty or hungry or even tired. The stale air had made him groggy. It seemed to press down on his skin and make his whole body feel numb.

At first the men had been able to stretch out, but the water slowly crept higher. Now they were huddled in a corner, hanging on to any available pipe or cable to avoid slipping into the water.

The compartment was quiet. Nobody wanted to use up precious oxygen by speaking or moving. Each man was wrapped up in his own thoughts. Occasionally someone would slip quietly to the edge of the water to urinate. Every now and then they turned on the flashlight to see whether the water level was rising.

It was.

The hours passed. George dozed. When he woke up, he was slumped against the side of the hull, his back resting against the shoulder of one of his shipmates. He was thinking about his family back in Annville. He wished he had written to his mother more often. He could picture her crying.

George shook his head. He didn't want to die. It could not all end now, just when things

Rescuers on the hull of the capsized *Oklahoma* attempt to free crewmembers trapped inside.

were getting good.

And then he heard something. They all did. It was a tapping sound. He listened hard. Was it coming from another compartment, just other guys sending out their own calls for help?

The tapping stopped. George's hope died.

Suddenly there was a new sound. It was the noise of cutting and drilling.

George held his breath. He heard a chunk of heavy metal drop and slide. There were distant voices. "Hooray, we're getting out!" The shouts were coming from men trapped in another compartment.

George didn't know what to feel. It wasn't that he didn't want the others to be rescued, but . . . what if help wasn't coming for them after all? What if their taps hadn't been heard?

The men all had the same thought. They started banging furiously on the bulkhead. The water level was so high, they knew they had very little time left.

Then the drilling noise started again, and this time it was right over their heads.

The compartment filled with the beam of a flashlight. They were looking up into a man's oil-stained face.

"Don't rush!" he shouted. He knew they would knock him over and send him sliding down the inner hull to his death if they all pushed forward at once.

George was scared now. As the air popped out of the compartment, there was no more pressure to hold back the water. He could see it rising quickly. Yet each man waited his turn, calmly, patiently.

"One at a time. Don't try to do anything, we'll get you out!" The rescuer lifted the first man out by his armpits like a baby and handed him to workers lined up behind him.

George was the fifth one out. The ragged metal from the holes that had been cut in the hull clawed his bare back, but he didn't even notice. When the fresh air hit his face, he took deep gulps. Then he stumbled across the hull and down to a waiting boat.

It was 4:00 Monday afternoon — thirty-two hours

since the first Japanese bomb had struck.

George felt as though he was walking out onto another planet. Pearl Harbor was transformed. The proud *Oklahoma* lay overturned like a beached whale, bleeding oil from the gaps in her hull. The *Arizona* was black and crumpled. Her mighty guns poked helplessly out of the sea. The water was an ugly stew of oil and floating debris, the air thick with smoke and the smell of burning fuel.

(Opposite) George is one of thirty-two men who are pulled out of the *Oklahoma* alive. (Above) The sight of the overturned *Okie* saddened many sailors, who had believed that a battleship could never capsize.

As the boat took them to a hospital ship, the rescued men peppered the coxswain with questions. He told them how the Japanese planes had suddenly appeared out of the clouds, dropping bombs and torpedoes. How a bomb had pierced the deck of the *Arizona*, setting off a million pounds of gunpowder. He told them how a Japanese plane had zoomed in over the *Oklahoma*, flying lower than the crow's nest before it released its torpedo. Their shipmates on deck had dived off the side when the ship rolled. Some had been crushed by sliding equipment; others had drowned in the oily water.

After the Japanese planes left, the rescue teams had cut holes in the sides of the battleship and listened for sounds of life within the hull. They had worked feverishly all night. When food was brought to them, the workers scooped it right out of the pot with their oil-stained hands, so as not to lose a minute of time.

Rescue boats had trawled the harbor under the moonlight, pulling oil-covered bodies out of the water like slippery fish. All through the night, nervous marines, sailors, and soldiers had scanned the horizon, waiting for the Japanese to return. They had even shot down five of their own planes in their panic.

In the hospital ship, George saw burned sailors from the *Arizona*. Some looked like human sticks of coal, charred and black. Others were burned raw, their skin pink and puffy.

That's when he knew how lucky he was. The attack was over, but for some, the nightmare was just beginning.

PILIALOHA: A HAWAIIAN GIRL'S STORY

In December 1941, fourteen-year-old Pilialoha Hopkins attended Kamehameha Schools, a Honolulu school for children of Hawaiian ancestry. (Today it is the second largest private school in America.) Pili still lives in Kaneohe on the island of Oahu.

In 1941 I had been a boarder at Kamehameha Schools for two years. At first I missed my family and our home in the little country town of Kaneohe. But many of the other students were away from home, too, and being homesick together made life easier for all of us.

On December 7 we woke up early and dressed in our church uniforms — "Sunday white" dresses with long silk stockings held up by old-fashioned garters. These garters were really not the best way to keep your stockings from rolling down your knees, and I was busy tugging at them as we headed off to church.

When I looked up, the blue skies were suddenly filled with patches of dark black clouds. I could hear rumbling and roaring that sounded like rifles and guns.

Everyone thought it was war games. But then we were quickly rushed back to our dormitories and given the news. We were at war!

We all cried as we clung to each other. The telephone system was completely blocked, so we could not reach our families. I was scared, comforted only by the fact that I was with my classmates.

In the afternoon we were each issued a strip of adhesive tape with our name printed on it. We were told to tape this to our shoulders. It was very frightening to think that we were being identified in case there were more bombs to come.

That same day a portion of the boys' school was turned into a temporary hospital. A huge red cross was painted on the roof. Ambulances brought in the injured. The wives and children of servicemen stationed on Oahu were brought up to our dormitories to stay. We did our best to comfort them. They were still in shock, wondering what had happened to their husbands and fathers. It was complete chaos.

Within a few days after the attack, all the students were sent home. At night complete blackouts were ordered. Everyone had to paint their windows with black paint or cover them with black tar paper so no light could be seen from the outside. Only emergency vehicles were allowed on the streets at night, and car headlights

Long lineups at the grocery stores became common. Windows were taped to prevent shattering in case of another attack.

were completely covered except for a tiny hole in the middle. Gasoline was rationed, and things like meat, mayonnaise, and butter were hard to find. There were often long lineups at the grocery stores. All silk went to make parachutes for the wartime pilots, so we could no longer buy stockings, either!

Since those years, my classmates have gone their separate ways. But whenever we can, we get together and reminisce about our days at Kamehameha. We do not talk about Pearl Harbor much anymore. Perhaps it is a part of our lives that we do not want to remember. Better still, we pray it will never happen again.

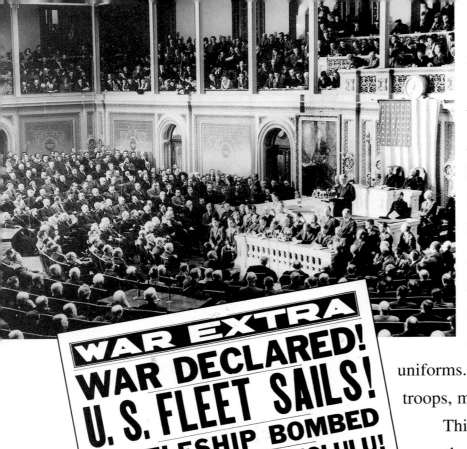

WAR EXTRA
WAR DECLARED!
U. S. FLEET SAILS!
BATTLESHIP BOMBED
2ND RAID ON HONOLULU!
America's Best Evening Newspaper
The Seattle Daily Times 3RD SUNDAY EXTRA!
PRICE FIVE CENTS
SEATTLE, WASHINGTON, MONDAY, DECEMBER 8, 1941.

(Top) President Roosevelt asks Congress to vote in favor of a war declaration against Japan. (Above) News of the attack made headlines all over the world. (Opposite) A draft of Roosevelt's message to Congress, with his hand-written changes, shows how carefully he chose his words.

It was the weekend, and Peter Nottage was going to the beach. Downtown Honolulu had changed. New businesses had opened up; Japanese shop signs had been taken down. You used to see older Japanese women in the streets in their kimonos and *geta*, but not anymore. Now the city was thick with American sailors and soldiers in their white and khaki uniforms. Every ship, it seemed, brought more troops, more defense workers from the mainland.

Things had happened quickly during the six months since the attack. Peter still remembered his mother waking him up to listen to the radio on the morning after the bombing. President Roosevelt was speaking, and his voice was full of steel: "Yesterday, December 7, 1941 — a date which will live in infamy — the United States of America was suddenly and deliberately attacked by naval and air forces of the Empire of Japan."

The United States was at war, and things were changed forever.

Peter walked from the bus stop to Waikiki Beach. These days you had to weave your way through barbed wire — protection against a possible invasion by the Japanese — just to reach the water. The sailors didn't seem to care about this obstacle. They lined the beach, sunning their pale bodies, roughhousing, and kicking sand at each other like a bunch of kids. Many of them didn't seem that much older than Peter.

Even the Royal Hawaiian Hotel had changed. Instead of glamorous tourists off the cruise ships, the pink-stucco building was filled with officers and government people.

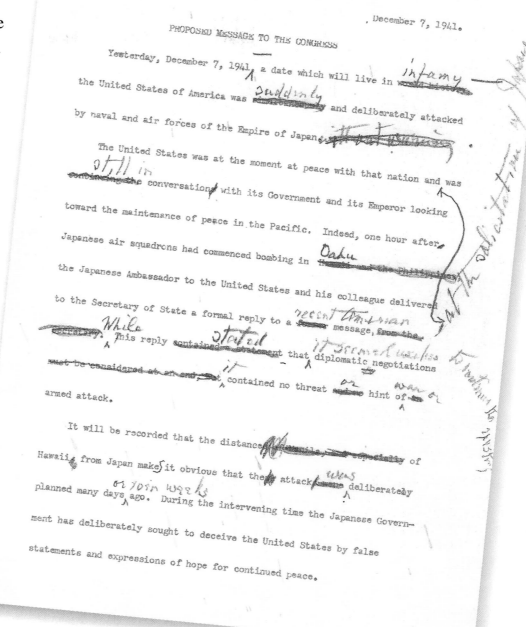

(Top) Waikiki Beach is strung with barbed wire in case of a Japanese invasion. (Above) A damaged schoolroom in Honolulu.

Peter looked for his fishermen friends, but they weren't around, either. He knew the new rules had been especially hard for them. How could they pull in their nets if the beaches were strung with barbed wire? How could they go night fishing, as they had always done, when the whole island was under strict curfew and the coastal waters were constantly patrolled?

Maybe he would round up some buddies and go diving. Sometimes they found spent cartridges and bomb casings that had landed in the water.

He decided to head back home, maybe help his mother in the garden. Lots of families were planting their own vegetables now — Victory Gardens, they were called. Everyone was encouraged to grow as much food as they could. Even the little kids helped. They called the weeds the enemies. The ones with the big roots were called the generals.

Everyone was doing whatever they could, making do with what they had. Back at Christmas, Peter and his brother had cut down an ironwood tree because the regular fir trees weren't being shipped from the mainland.

At first, school had been canceled for several weeks. When it did start up again, classes were held in churches and people's living rooms for a while. Nobody learned very much, but the grown-ups were all busy and preoccupied and the kids needed something to do. The engineer corps had taken over Punahou School. Peter had earned twenty-five cents an hour carting belongings out of the dorms. It felt like a fortune.

When real classes began again, there were regular air-raid drills. At the sound of the siren, all the students would jump into the trenches that had been dug around the building. The blackout rules continued. The Nottages nailed tar paper over all their windows. When Peter peeked out at night, all of Honolulu was pitch black.

Everyone was issued gas masks in case of a poison-gas attack. There were drills to see how quickly they could get the masks out of their cases and over their faces. The little kids were taught breath-holding games. They pretended they were smelling bad medicine, while they hurried to a gasproof room. Peter and his father dug a bomb shelter in the

(Above) Peter plays in his family's makeshift bunker. (Top right) Two young Americans help out on a plantation due to a shortage of workers.

People wait at the cablegram office to send messages to loved ones on the mainland.

backyard. It was pretty small — like a very big grave. He couldn't imagine having to stay in it, but he helped his mother stock it with candles, canned food, blankets, and water.

Peter knew that things were worse for other people. He had heard that some Japanese Americans were being sent to internment camps, and he couldn't understand why. He said good-bye to his brothers and neighbors who were drafted into the service. Some of his friends had moved to the mainland, and Peter wondered whether his family would leave, too. His mother had been told that New Mexico was a safe place. It was about as far away from an ocean and harbor as you could get.

It was time to walk back to the bus stop. These days there were often lineups.

Peter took a deep breath. The air was heavy with the scent of oleander. A mynah bird called. He took one last look at the beach. The sea breezes were as soft as ever, the ocean still turquoise and blue.

He hoped they wouldn't have to leave. After all, Hawaii was his home.

DANIEL INOUYE'S STORY

In December 1941, Dan Inouye was a typical seventeen-year-old American teenager. He went to McKinley High in downtown Honolulu. He played baseball and sang in the church choir. He listened to Benny Goodman songs and volunteered at the Red Cross.

As soon as he heard news of the attack, Dan reported for work at the Red Cross. American antiaircraft fire, aimed at the Japanese planes, had rained down on Honolulu, setting buildings on fire all over the downtown. Dan dragged the injured from burning homes and treated their wounds. He collected the remains of the dead and carried them to the morgue. He helped dazed people find their families. He did not go home for five days.

He continued to work after the immediate crisis was over, going to school in the morning and working a twelve-hour shift at the Red Cross every night. It was exhausting, but he was proud and grateful to be able to help. It was, he thought, what any loyal American would do.

So it was a surprise to him to learn that not everyone considered him a loyal American. His grandparents had come from Japan to work in the sugar cane fields. His hair was black, and his eyes slanted. He looked just like the enemy. Some thought he must be the enemy.

Things got worse for the 150,000 Japanese Americans who lived in Hawaii. Their radios and cameras were seized. Japanese-language schools were closed, and Japanese newspapers were censored. Homes were searched without warrants.

Two months after the attack on Pearl Harbor, the U.S. government declared that all Americans of Japanese ancestry were enemy agents. On the mainland, in both the United States and Canada, people of Japanese descent were herded into camps surrounded by barbed wire. They lost their homes, businesses, and possessions. But very few were interned in Hawaii, where almost forty percent of the population was of Japanese origin. To remove them would have brought the economy to a standstill and created chaos.

Young Japanese Americans on the islands eventually had a chance to prove their loyalty many times over. In 1943, Dan Inouye was one of 2,600 volunteers (chosen from 9,500) who fought heroically in Europe with the 442nd Regimental Combat Team. He lost an arm in battle and came home with fifteen medals and citations, including the Purple Heart and Distinguished Service Cross. He became a U.S. senator in 1962. In May 2000, he was awarded the Congressional Medal of Honor for gallantry in World War II.

Epilogue

Peter (second from left) and his family in April 1942, just before the women and children left for the safety of the mainland. (Opposite) Peter Nottage today.

Peter Nottage and his family did end up moving to the mainland. The military encouraged all women and children to leave, as the islands would be easier to defend with fewer people. The Nottages returned to Hawaii before the end of the war. Peter now lives in Kaneohe.

George DeLong today.

Not many men on the *Oklahoma* were as lucky as George DeLong. More than four hundred crewmembers died.

On board the hospital ship, George was given a clean bill of health, a meal, and a bed for the night. The next day he reported for duty at the receiving station and was reassigned to the USS *Helena*. He eventually returned to the mainland for further assignment, but even then the attack lay heavy on everyone's mind. As the *Helena* took a northerly route to San Francisco, the men suddenly reported seeing several enemy submarines. After a few minutes they realized they had sailed into a pod of seals, their shiny black noses poking out of the water like periscopes.

KAZUO SAKAMAKI
ISN HJ 1 MI

KAZUO SAKAMAKI
ISN HJ 1 MI

Kazuo Sakamaki was captured on the southeast coast of Oahu, about fifteen miles from Pearl Harbor. He was the only one of the ten midget-sub crewmembers to survive. The others were given dignified military funerals and hailed as heroes in Japan. It was Sakamaki's shame to be known as the first prisoner of war taken by the United States.

Sakamaki spent four years in American prison camps. During that time, the war in the Pacific gradually turned against Japan. The attack on Pearl Harbor killed 2,388 people, and it shocked the Americans into entering the war with will and a vengeance. Most of the damaged warships were repaired, and American victories began to mount. Finally, in August 1945, the United States dropped atomic bombs on the cities of Hiroshima and Nagasaki, killing more than 200,000 people. Japan was in ruins, and the country quickly surrendered.

(Top) Kazuo Sakamaki's prisoner identification photos. (Above) Sakamaki visits his sub on display at the Nimitz Museum in Fredericksburg, Texas, in 1991.

After Pearl Harbor, Mitsuo Fuchida returned to active service and narrowly escaped death several times during the war. His plane was shot down over Borneo and he spent three days wandering through the jungle, tying himself to tree limbs at night to avoid being attacked by wild animals. Eventually he clutched a log and floated down a crocodile-infested river to safety. During the Battle of Midway, his aircraft carrier was bombed. When he attempted to abandon ship, an explosion hurled him ten feet down a deck, breaking both his ankles and setting his clothes on fire. And at the end of the war, Fuchida was sent to Hiroshima to report on the horrific damage caused by the atomic bomb. He spent three days wading through the radioactive rubble and was the only one of eleven men in the group who did not die of radiation poisoning.

Japan never did launch another full-scale attack on Hawaii. After the war, many experts agreed with Fuchida that the Japanese should have gone back to take out the U.S. submarine bases, repair shops, fuel tanks, and electrical supply. Such a move, they argued, might well have changed the course of the war.

Every year, at 7:55 a.m. on December 7, boats gather in Pearl Harbor and people toss flowers into the water in memory of the attack. The *Arizona*, the battleship on which 1,177 men died, is now a war grave and memorial that more than 1.5 million visitors, including many Japanese, visit each year.

THE *ARIZONA* MEMORIAL

Today the USS *Arizona* lies in forty feet of water and is spanned by a white concrete structure that looks like a bridge (above). This monument was dedicated on Memorial Day 1962. (Top right) Visitors can read the names of *Arizona's* 1,177 dead on a white marble wall in the memorial's shrine room. (Left) Fuel oil still seeps from the *Arizona's* remains into the waters of Pearl Harbor.

...we here highly resolve that these dead shall not have died in vain...

REMEMBER DEC. 7th!

HAWAII
REMEMBER PEARL HARBOR

HELP AMERICA WIN THE WAR
TWO
DIRECT HITS
RECEIVES ONE TEN CENT DEFENSE STAMP
DROP COIN HERE

Civilian DEFENSE

BUY
DEFENSE SAVINGS STAMPS
HERE

REMEMBER PEARL HARBOR

REMEMBER PEARL HARBOR

"Remember Pearl Harbor" became the rallying cry of Americans. Posters, decals, clothing, pins, plates, dolls, games, and many other items all bore the message that no one should ever forget the attack on Pearl Harbor — the day America entered World War II.

Glossary

antiaircraft guns: Guns used on a ship or on the ground for defense against enemy airplanes.

bulkhead: A wall or partition inside a ship.

caliber: The diameter of a bullet or shell.

carrier: A ship with a flat top deck used for carrying aircraft.

coxswain: The steersman of a boat.

foremast: The upright pole at the front of a ship, used to hold radio aerials, flags, or sails.

fuselage: The central part of an airplane's body that holds the crew and passengers or cargo.

geta: Traditional Japanese wooden shoes worn outdoors.

gyrocompass: A special compass with a gyroscope or spinning axis that can find true north even when subjected to movement. It is used to help direct and steer a ship.

magazine: The room on a ship where explosives are stored.

martial law: Government or rule by the armed forces, temporarily suspending ordinary law. This military rule is enforced during times of danger or emergency.

quartermaster striker: A petty or noncommissioned naval officer who attends to the ship's helm or wheel and signals. In the Navy, a "striker" is a seaman preparing for a rank.

Index

Picture Credits

All illustrations are by David Craig unless otherwise indicated. All maps are by Jack McMaster. Every effort has been made to attribute correctly all material reproduced in this book. If any errors have unwittingly occurred, we will be happy to correct them in future editions.

Back cover: (Bottom right) © CORBIS

4: Courtesy of Peter Nottage

5: (Left) Brown Brothers; (Top right) © Lake County Museum/CORBIS; (Middle and bottom right) Bishop's Museum

7: Courtesy of Peter Nottage

8: U.S. Naval Institute

9: (Bottom) © Yogi, Inc./CORBIS

10: Admiral Nimitz National Museum of the Pacific War

12: Naval Historical Center NH 91337

13: Courtesy of George DeLong

14: © Bettmann/CORBIS

15: Brown Brothers

19: (Top) Naval Historical Center NH 98442; (Middle) National Archives 80-G-71198; (Bottom) United States Air Force Art Collection

23: Naval Historical Center NH 50929

25: Naval Historical Center NH 50931

28: (Top left) National Archives; (Bottom left) © CORBIS; (Right, top and bottom) National Archives

30: Courtesy of Peter Nottage

36: (Top) National Archives 80-G-32586; (Bottom) Brown Brothers

37: (Top) National Archives 80-G-36822; (Bottom) © Bettmann/CORBIS

38: (Top left) Naval Historical Center NH 50926; (Top right) U.S. Naval Institute; (Bottom left) Naval Historical Center NH 50473; (Bottom right) Brown Brothers

39: (Inset) U.S. Naval Institute

42: (Top) National Archives 80-G-17079; (Bottom) Admiral Nimitz National Museum of the Pacific War

43: National Archives 111-SC-234135

46: National Archives 80-G-19941

49: National Archives 80-G-32741

50: Courtesy of Pilialoha and John Oliver

51: Brown Brothers

52: (Top) National Archives 208-PP-129-1; (Bottom) Naval Historical Center SC-234135

53: Courtesy of the FDR Library

54: (Top) Brown Brothers; (Bottom) © Bettmann/CORBIS

55: (Top right) © Pan Pacific Press Bureau/Bishop's Museum; (Bottom left) Courtesy of Peter Nottage

56: Brown Brothers

57: Courtesy of Daniel Inouye

58: (Top left) Courtesy of Peter Nottage; (Top right) © Peter Christopher; (Bottom left) Courtesy of George DeLong

59: (Top and bottom) Admiral Nimitz National Museum of the Pacific War

60-61: © Peter Christopher

62: (Top left) Naval Historical Center NH 72273 KN; (Top right) Bishop's Museum; (Bottom left and right) Courtesy of Martin S. Jacobs

63-64: Courtesy of Martin S. Jacobs

Acknowledgments

The text of this book, including any dialogue, is based on the first-person accounts written by Mitsuo Fuchida, Daniel Inouye, and Kazuo Sakamaki, and on interviews provided by George DeLong, Peter Nottage, and Pilialoha Oliver.

The author and Madison Press Books would like to thank George DeLong, John Lundstrom, Ainslie Manson, Peter Nottage, Pilialoha and John Oliver, Sandi Skousen, and John Treiber.